ershi

CESAR CASTELLANOS D.

leadership

DOCTRINE

LEVEL 3

TEACHERS' GUIDE

leader

G12 editors

Published by G12 Editores
sales@g12bookstore.com

ISBN 1-932285-23-7

Made in Colombia

Printed in Colombia

CONTENTS

FORWARD

The emphasis of this, the 3rd, workbook in the School of Leaders, is on leadership. The main objective of this volume is to "endow every person that is willing to be used by God in the vision of cells and in the model of the twelve. With these basic guidelines it should be easier to develop an effective leadership that contributes to the strengthening of the leader's ministry and the growth of the Church."

One of the most important commitments we have made before God is "to make every believer a leader." All believers, whether children, young people, men or women, are potential leaders. They all must develop the character of Christ in order to experience how the Lord levels out those rough places in their lives. All are gifted to some degree, yes, but the goal is that they are placed in God's hands to be formed into effective instruments for the kingdom of God. His kingdom must be established in every life and as soon as we begin the task of helping them to accomplish this, we too can say "for the earth will be filled with the knowledge of the glory of the Lord, as the waters cover the sea" (Habakkuk 2:14).

All students who attend the Third Level of the School of Leaders, now have a simple, practical workbook that guides them into becoming leaders according to God's own heart as well as to the demands of this modern world so that they will be able to meet the current needs of the Church.

Teachers and students, who will apply the principles in this workbook, will be able to experience an inner growth, which will then be reflected externally, since this leads to a successful leadership.

Cesar Castellanos D.

Leadership

1
LESSON

TEACHING OBJECTIVE

The student must understand the concept of leadership, its characteristics, and its importance in the ministry.

STUDENT OBJECTIVE

1 The student must be able to define what leadership is.

2 The student must be able to explain the characteristics of a leader of success.

BIBLICAL FOUNDATIONAL REFERENCE

Matthew 5:1-16

CORRESPONDING BIBLICAL FOUNDATION

Mark 9:35

Hebrews 11

1 Corinthians 11:1

2 Timothy 2:15;

1 Samuel 17:45-46

Acts 13:1-3

2 Timothy 2:1-2

KEY VERSE

"You are the salt of the earth. But if the salt loses its saltiness, how can it be made salty again? It is no longer good for anything, except to be thrown out and trampled by men" **(Matthew 5:13).**

PURPOSE

When people asked the great Master Michelangelo about his masterpiece "David", he said: "The image was always there, the only thing I did was remove some debris to discover it."

The same has happened with the leadership model of the twelve.
It has always been there only the Lord has allowed us to remove some debris, which prevented the believers to see it clearly.

Through the model of the twelve we have been able to discover the potential of hundreds and hundreds of people who come to our church. With the guidance of the Holy Spirit, they have been molded becoming leaders who bear extraordinary fruit.

In other words, the model of the twelve has helped to identify the true concept of leadership and to apply it effectively in the work of our ministry.

The purpose of this lesson is to help you know the essence of leadership from a biblical perspective and guide you to discover the leader that is in you and help the students do so, too.

1. WHAT IS LEADERSHIP?

There are numerous definitions and concepts about leadership, but it is fundamental that this be formed at the foot of the cross since there is where man sets aside sin, pride, arrogance, selfishness, greed, etc. In this manner we will be prepared to exercise influence on others and help them reach the development of their highest potential.

Influence covers three essential aspects:

Molding a person's character, discovering their talents, and recognizing their worth. Having this in mind about the person allows the leader to begin the process of guiding him towards his personal realization. In meeting the responsibility of this task, you will be considered a successful leader.

A. Leading others

If you have already succeeded in cultivating an excellent relationship with the Holy Spirit, who is the best friend that you can have, you are already being properly influenced. Receiving directives from above makes it easy to carry them out.

The centurion, who longed for his servant to be healed, made it clear that he understood authority when he said to the Lord, "Lord, I do not deserve to have you come under my roof. But just say the word, and my servant will be healed. For I myself am a man under authority, with soldiers under me. I tell this one, 'Go,' and he goes; and that one, 'Come,' and he comes. I say to my servant, 'Do this,' and he does it.' When Jesus heard this, he was astonished and said to those following him, "I tell you the truth, I have not found anyone in Israel with such great faith" (Matthew 8:7-10).

Jesus said, "you are the salt of the earth". But if the salt loses its saltiness, how can it be made salty again? It is no longer good for anything, except to be thrown out and trampled by men (Matthew 5:13).

Integrity must be the foundation of leadership. When you forfeit integrity it is like selling your first-born rights for a bowl of bean stew. Don't underestimate the worth of standing in righteousness because in so doing, the heart develops in accordance to God's heart.

You must be blameless before the LORD your God (Deuteronomy 18:13).

"But just as he who called you is holy, so be holy in all you do" (1 Peter 1:15).

"...a broken and contrite heart, O God, you will not despise" (Psalm 51:17).

"My ears had heard of you but now my eyes have seen you. Therefore I despise myself and repent in dust and ashes" (Job 42:5-6).

"Consider it pure joy, my brothers, whenever you face trials of many kinds, because you know that the testing of your faith develops perseverance." James 1:2-3.

B. Encouraging others

People are most motivated when they know where they are going, when they can see progress in their ministry and when they can clearly see a way to accomplish their goals.

As Jesus led His disciples, His leadership consisted of constant motivation. He never ceased to encourage them so that they could fulfill the desire of their hearts by means of having a good will, a correct attitude, and diligence.

He was able to give such consistent encouragement because he had permanent contact with them, showing himself as the example.

The leader that wants to attain success with his disciples should not be jealous or distrustful, for the goal of the leader is to help them develop into their maximum potential. Thanks to the motivation the Lord gave to his disciples, they put forth great effort to spread the doctrine through out the entire world, offering their lives because of Christ.

The influence of true leadership encourages and motivates the individual, pushing him to be innovative yet advices him when he is tempted to exploit his gifts and talents. But above all, the leader trains the disciple until he has the ability to influence others.

The apostle Paul said, "Follow my example, as I follow the example of Christ" (1 Corinthians 11:1).

Influence is the ability to get followers. Nobody can say that he is a leader unless he has someone following him. In other words, "the one who thinks he is leading and has nobody following him is merely going for a walk."

C. Fostering personal development.

With a specific vision in mind, true leadership contributes to the personal development of every one who is being led, understanding that the fulfillment of this purpose depends on the integrity of the leader.

Concerning this matter, Paul said to Timothy, "Do your best to present yourself to God as one approved, a workman who does not need to be ashamed and who correctly handles the word of truth" (2 Timothy 2:15).

The true leader desires a positive change for those who are under him. A firm leadership cares for their follower's interests and for. The improvement in their lifestyles.

D. Forging courageous people.

Effective leadership is made up of valiant people, those who have overcome fears, insecurity, complexes, and the like. It will be these conquerors that will be able to forge these like kinds onto their teams. God's strategy to forge his valiant ones is the same, He always tries His people through little things first, and He does not give big responsibilities until He is certain that we will be able to take them on.

David is a clear example of a leader who was shaped by small events who then became a brave man in God's hands. Having been trained in his work as a shepherd, often facing the wild beasts, the time came when he was able to face a giant. David challenged him, absolutely convinced that He who had saved him from the wild beasts would also save him from the giant. In the name of the Lord he would obtain victory (1 Samuel 17:45-46).

2. IDEAL PURPOSE OF LEADERSHIP

To spread the vision. We know that the most powerful way to effectively spread the vision is through the government of the twelve, just as the Lord Jesus did. It is the leader's duty to pass the vision down to every one in his team, making sure to relay it clearly so that they too may do the same for those they are leading. We believe, in this way, the leader's character is being formed in order to fulfill the purpose that God designed for his life such as:

a. Having a correct self-image.

"But I do not think I am in the least inferior to those 'super-apostles.' I may not be a trained speaker, but I do have knowledge. We have made this perfectly clear to you in every way" (2 Corinthians 11:5-6).

b. Being an example to others.

"You love righteousness and hate wickedness; therefore God, your God, has set you above your companions by anointing you with the oil of joy" (Psalm 45:7).

c. Living in the Word.

"Do not let this Book of the Law depart from your mouth; meditate on it day and night, so that you may be careful to do everything written in it. Then you will be prosperous and successful" (Joshua 1:8).

d. Being teachable towards God.

"I will instruct you and teach you in the way you should go; I will counsel you and watch over you" (Psalm 32:8).

e. Being able to teach your family.

"As for me, this is my covenant with them," says the LORD. "My Spirit, who is in you, and my words that I have put in your mouth will not depart from your mouth, or from the mouths of your children, or from the mouths of their descendants from this time on and forever," says the LORD (Isaiah 59:21).

f. Having a pastor's heart.

"And David shepherded them with integrity of heart; with skillful hands he led them" (Psalm 78:72).

g. Having your own team of twelve.

"Solomon also had twelve district governors over all of Israel, who supplied provisions for the king and the royal household. Each one had to provide supplies for one month in the year" (1 Kings 4:7).

"Give him "the team" some of your authority so the whole Israelite community will obey him" (Numbers 27:20).

"Choose some wise, understanding and respected men from each of your tribes, and I will set them over you" (Deuteronomy 1:13).

CONCLUSION

A good leader will have a positive influence on his followers without fail. He will help them to develop a new mindset that will lead them to change their entire lifestyle. A good leader should not become tired of monitoring the development of his followers. If you want to become a successful leader, you will embrace dreams; have specific goals and absolute commitment. This is what fulfills our purpose of spreading the vision.

APPLICATION

1. Set out in your heart to be the best leader in the world.
2. Cultivate friendship with the Holy Spirit.
3. Constantly live motivated in order to motivate others.
4. If you are already a leader, study the characteristics of a successful leader as described in this lesson. Strengthen those areas in which you find personal deficiencies.

EVALUATION

Due to the importance of the subject on leadership, it is imperative that each objective is thoroughly evaluated. This may be done by way of a quiz or homework that will be verified. It is necessary for the student to know what the bible says about successful leadership.

RECOMMENDATIONS

Bibliographical

SUCCESFUL LEADERSHIP THROUGH THE GOVERNMENT OF 12, by Pastor Cesar Castellanos.

Biblical

Read the gospels and learn about the leadership of Jesus Christ in order to obtain a clearer picture.

Methodological

Questions and answers will be helpful for the development of this lesson. Rouse an interest among the students for a deeper study into the biblical foundation of leadership. Use visual aids to explain the subjects.

STUDENTS' ASSIGNMENT

Read chapters 2 and 3 of part 1 of the book SUCCESFUL LEADERSHIP THROUGH THE GOVERNMENT OF 12 by Pastor Cesar Castellanos, and make a summary to be handed in to your instructor.

Focus this assignment on your life as a leader.

The Calling

2
LESSON

TEACHING OBJECTIVE

The student must understand the importance of the calling of God for his life.

STUDENT OBJECTIVE

1 The student must be able to explain the biblical foundation for the calling.

2 The student must be able to explain what the calling is.

3 The student must be able to explain the characteristics of the calling.

BIBLICAL FOUNDATIONAL REFERENCE

Jeremiah 1:4-10

CORRESPONDING BIBLICAL FOUNDATION

Romans 11:29

2 Timothy 1:9

Philippians 3:14

2 Thessalonians 1:11

Hebrews 3:1

Ephesians 4:11

Exodus 18:21

KEY VERSE

"Before I formed you in the womb I knew you, before you were born I set you apart; I appointed you as a prophet to the nations"
(Jeremiah 1:5)

PURPOSE

The student must understand the importance of the vision of the government of 12 because it is integrated into the calling. We must understand that whenever God gives a vision, we should join efforts in order to make it grow because each one of us was chosen before the foundation of the world.

The purpose of this lesson is that you may recognize God's calling on your life and how to respond effectively to it, so that you may be molded and used by the Lord.

In order to carry out His purpose here on earth, God always chooses to use a man or a woman. When He wanted to free his people from the oppression they were suffering in Egypt, He chose Moses; He formed him and then sent him to his people, so that he would take them out of Egypt. Then, God surrounded Moses with people who believed in his calling and were willing to support him in every decision he had to make.

When the Lord Jesus was here on earth, He chose twelve men, whom he called apostles. Jesus invested most of his ministerial life in these men, and then He sent them on to continue with the redeeming mission He had begun.

1. WHAT IS THE CALLING ?

Even though Jesus could have poured his life out to the multitudes, He didn't.
He preferred to work skillfully, shaping the character of twelve persons who were completely different from each other. Like the potter with the clay, for three and a half years Jesus molded the character of each one of them, and then, He breathed on them and said, "Receive the Holy Spirit" (John 20:2-22).

How could Jesus have taken twelve persons without any culture, education, riches or social position, encourage and develop them so, that they ultimately became the pillars of Christianity? The answer is simple. These people responded to the calling of God, and were willing to be molded by him, so that, they would be sent out.
"And we know that all things work together for the good of those who love Him, who have been called according to His purpose" (Romans 8:28).

In the vision God gave us through the government of the twelve, we can see that all the people in our communities are potential leaders. Once they go through the process of formation in a short time, they will be able to see fruit in their life. Jesus had to leave his disciples a model for their lives, in which they were able to project themselves. Paul said, "Follow my example, as I follow the example of Christ" (Corinthians 11:1). "And I tell you that you are Peter, and on this rock I will build my church, and the gates of Hades will not overcome it" (Matthew 16:18).

The Church the Lord was referring to was the one made up of people from every culture, race, and social class. Simply because they believe in Him, they are a part of His body. Those are the ones the Lord calls, 'my church', because they are part of Him.

People are the church. Therefore our task is to win and to work! Just as Jesus did with His apostles, we must work with each one very carefully and win them over. "You also, like living stones, are being built into a spiritual house to be a holy priesthood" (1 Peter 2:5). In order to build, one must first dig deeply.

Even though the Lord did not have a temple, multitudes followed Him because they knew He had the answers to their needs. This moved him to put together a group of twelve, so that all the people could be pastored in a personal way.

> The government of twelve has always been in God's heart. What is the secret of the twelve? God made it clear to me years ago. I could hear, in the bottom of my heart, the voice of the Holy Spirit saying, "if you train twelve people and succeed in reproducing in them the character of Christ that is already in you, and if every one of them does the same with another twelve, and if they do the same with yet another twelve, getting them to have the same conviction, you and your church will experience an unprecedented growth." In my mind, I immediately began to see the projected growth of my ministry, and I knew that it would not take long.

2. RECOGNIZE THE CALLING

Sensitivity to the Holy Spirit is one of the conditions that are essential in order to hear God's calling and understand it. We are aware of the fact that we are not in the ministry because of our gifts, talents, or skills, but by God's grace toward each one of us; "But to each one of us grace has been given as Christ apportioned it" (Ephesians 4:7). When we are sensitive to the Holy Spirit, the gifts begin to be effective in our lives. "It was he who gave some to be apostles, some to be prophets, some to be evangelists, and some to be pastors and teachers, to prepare God's people for works of service, so that the body of Christ may be built up" (Ephesians 4:11-12). These five ministries are the extension of the character of Christ in us.

Acknowledging God's call involves the following:

A. Conviction

It is essential to have absolute certainty that God has called us into the ministry, coupled with the correct motivation, in order to go into ministry. Why? It would be impossible to develop a supernatural work with a natural attitude and motivation. Besides, we know that whom God calls He will also equip in all things.

B. Commitment

The fact is God chose you from among the millions of humans dwelling here on planet earth. You were selected by him to continue His work. "Whom shall I send? And who will go for us?" And I said, "Here am I. Send me!" (Isaiah 6:8). God could have chosen someone else, but He preferred to choose you. Now, go and do God's work without fear.

C. Brokenness

"I tell you the truth, unless a kernel of wheat falls to the ground and dies, it remains only a single seed. But if it dies, it produces many seeds" (John 12:24). The apostle Paul was a person who has experienced brokenness, and he did not consider his life precious. He just wanted to finish his assignment successfully. Brokenness is the most powerful protection mechanism a believer can have while facing the adversities of life.

D. Anointing

This is when you experience the presence of God in your life continuously. It is reflected in the way you speak, in what you teach, in what you pray, in what you understand and in the people you lead. "The Spirit of the LORD came upon him in power. The ropes on his arms became like charred flax, and the bindings dropped from his hands" (Judges 15:14).

Samson seemed to be like anybody else, the difference was that he had God's anointing. God gave us the anointing for us to develop His work effectively.

E. Submission

Those who are in spiritual authority must understand that our authority over others is not an imposition but a posture of managing others as we present ourselves as examples in every thing. "And the disciples will accept and at the same time exert the authority in a correct way, without hurting people"
(Romans 13:1-2)

F. Fruitfulness

One of the great advantages this vision has is that everybody can develop all the potential he has inside, because it is reflected in fruitfulness. I know that there is no greater joy for a person than feeling useful in the work of the Lord. "So you also, when you have done everything you were told to do, should say, 'We are unworthy servants; we have only done our duty.'"
(Luke 17:10)

CONCLUSION

The Lord has assigned a mission to you. "I looked for a man among them who would build up the wall and stand before me in the gap on behalf of the land so I would not have to destroy it, but I found none" (Ezekiel 22:30). Be faithful to God's calling, He has His eyes fixed on you.

God assigns us specific tasks in His work. This calling is in line with God's purpose for every believer. The accomplishment of the call depends on the fulfillment of the requirements established in the Scriptures, such as the ones stated in Exodus 18:21.

APPLICATION

1. Have absolute certainty of your calling.
2. Share your faith in Christ with others. God's anointing is in your life.
3. Intensify your daily prayer level, until you feel the fire of the Spirit burning in you.
4. Pray for your team of twelve.
5. Dream of the multitudes being born from your heart and believe that God will bring them to you.
6. Discover what gifting or talents you possess and conse crate them to serve the Lord.

EVALUATION

Use questions/answers to check the students understanding of the calling.

RECOMMENDATIONS

Bibliographical

SUCCESFUL LEADERSHIP THROUGH THE GOVERNMENT OF 12, by Pastor Cesar Castellanos D.

DREAM AND YOU WILL WIN THE WORLD, by Pastor Cesar Castellanos D.

Biblical

In the Bible there are many examples of men of God who were called with a specific purpose. Study some of them in order to use them in the lesson.

STUDENTS' ASSIGNMENT

Read chapters 1 and 2 of part 1 of the book DREAM AND YOU WILL WIN THE WORLD by Pastor Cesar Castellanos, and make a summary to be handed in to your instructor.
Focus this assignment on your life as a leader.

The Personality of the Leader
Part 1

3
LESSON

TEACHING OBJECTIVE

The student must understand the need of maturity in order to be a person of good of character.

STUDENT OBJECTIVE

1 The student must be able to define what personality is and its importance in leadership.

2 The student must be able to explain the characteristics of the leader's personality.

BIBLICAL FOUNDATIONAL REFERENCE

Galatians 5:22, 23

1 Timothy 3:1-10

CORRESPONDING BIBLICAL FOUNDATION

Titus 1:5-7

2 Timothy 2:15

1 Thessalonians 5:23

Psalm 139:13

1 Corinthians 13

Galatians 5:16

Romans 5:3-5

Romans 14:17

John 14:27

Luke 6:27-31

Mark 10:17-18

Hebrews 11:1-6

1 Corinthians 9:24-27

KEY VERSE

"But the fruit of the Spirit is love, joy, peace, patience, kindness, goodness, faithfulness, gentleness and self-control"
(Galatians 5:22, 23)

PURPOSE

The world desperately longs for leaders who have an honest heart, who can be real examples before others not only in the position of preachers, but also as men who are leaders in their homes; men of truth, people of character. One of the greatest assets of the model of the twelve is the focus on molding the character of a leader.

The purpose of this lesson is to guide the student to effectively understand the concept of personality and its importance in the life of a leader.

1. PERSONALITY

We may ask ourselves what God had in mind when He decided to create man. There is no doubt that he visualized a being that would be able to reproduce His character and His will. For this reason, we know why He blew His breath of life into man's nostrils; as He rules over heaven, He wanted man to rule over the things on earth. God reproduced His character in the human being for such reasons as Paul stated, "For we are God's workmanship, created in Christ Jesus to do good works, which God prepared in advance for us to do" (Ephesians 2:10).

God designed a righteous, loving, happy man, who was able to have fellowship and live in a society, who could enjoy a permanent and intimate relationship with his Creator. Man´s personality used to be the same as God´s. What lays on the inside of a person shows in their actions. The Lord uses the trees as an example; if the tree is good, it will produce good fruits; if the tree is bad it will produce bad fruits. If a person is full of God, he will show it through good actions. On the other hand, the person who is not full of God will show whatever he has allowed to be in his mind and heart; everything within a person is reflected through his actions.

As a rule, a life controlled by the Holy Spirit has solid principles, correct attitudes, and self-control. Someone's personality must reflect the fruit of the Spirit that the person has inside. "But the fruit of the Spirit is love, joy, peace, patience, kindness, goodness, faithfulness, gentleness and self-control" (Galatians 5:22, 23).

Being a person of character comes from understanding the redeeming work of the cross. There is where all our debts were cancelled, all our sins were erased, all our failures were banished and we were redeemed from the curse. Understanding and accepting the redeeming work is recovering our identity.

A. Temperament

This has to do with our inner person. It is what makes every person unique, distinguishing them from any other person. There are four basic temperaments proposed by Hippocrates:

- Sanguine: Enthusiastic, vigorous and athletic.

- Choleric: A born leader but tends to get angry easily.

- Melancholic: Tends to be calm but may fall in depression and sadness.

- Phlegmatic: Very easy going but seems to be tired more often than not.

All servants of God were molded in their own temperaments until reaching the point of balance. Moses' temperament was so strong that on one occasion he killed an Egyptian and later buried him so that no one would know it. God's dealings with him were so effective that He became the meekest and most humble man on earth (Numbers 12:3).

B. Character

It is the external reflection of what we have accepted internally. It is said that temperament and character make up the personality of a human being. Pharaoh was hard and obstinate, his advisers were in the occult. As a result, demons were able to subtly enter him and control his character. When the Lord came to the earth, He presented Himself as a Teacher of excellence. He said, "...and learn from me, for I am gentle and humble in heart, and you will find rest for your souls" (Matthew 11:29).

Jesus is the only one who can have a positive influence on the development of our character and when He governs our lives, He will take charge and remove any negative influence from our past. We reveal Jesus to the world by what we are.

2. FUNDAMENTAL ATTITUDES THAT WILL HELP US GROW

a. Feed your faith daily

We know that faith comes by hearing the Word of God. It is active and reaches only those people who have decided to understand the Word of God. Learning to live in faith lifts us above circumstances, enabling us to move in this world according to what we see happening in the spiritual realm. Our strength comes as we continually confess the word of the promise given to us by God. "For everyone born of God overcomes the world. This is the victory that has overcome the world, even our faith" (1 John 5:4).

b. Be a well-balanced person.

Avoiding the extremes is essential. Paul gives some advice to Timothy (1 Timothy 4:12-16):

- Be an example, with your words, with your conduct and with your love.
- Devote yourself to reading, exhorting and teaching.
- Do not neglect the spiritual gift which is in you.
- Watch your life and the doctrine.

c. Get your family involved in the ministry

This will be prime protection against any attack from the adversary. We know that God is restoring the priestly family anointing to those committed to the ministry; this vision contributes to the development of your whole family.

- A calling to the family
  "'You will be for me a kingdom of priests and a holy nation.' These are the words you are to speak to the Israelites" (Exodus 19:6).

- An anointing of restoration
  "He will turn the hearts of the fathers to their children, and the hearts of the children to their fathers; or else I will come and strike the land with a curse" (Malachi 4:6).

- A leader who sets the example
  "And it will be, like people, like priests. I will punish both of them for their ways and repay them for their deeds" (Hosea 4:9).

CONCLUSION

You are God's masterpiece; Christ's character has been reproduced in you, and you have the ability to be self-controlled. Know your temperament; make the daily effort of submitting every area of your life to the control of the Holy Spirit, thus reflecting the fruit of the Spirit; because you will have that uniqueness, which in turn, grants to you authority as you become active in the ministry.

APPLICATION

1. Analyze your behavior compared to other people's behavior and try to discover the most predominant features of your personality until you can define your prevailing temperament.

2. According to Galatians 5: 22-23, notice the characteristics which make up your leadership style, and if you find weaknesses in some areas, strengthen them in prayer with the guidance of your leader.

EVALUATION

Ask the student to take 5 minutes to write down the weaknesses of his character and the way he thinks that he can change them.

RECOMMENDATIONS

Bibliographical

Intensify your knowledge about this subject by reading the books:

SUCCESFUL LEADERSHIP THROUGH THE GOVERNMENT OF 12, SUBMERGED IN HIS SPIRIT (from the series as firm As the Rock) by Pastor Cesar Castellanos Dominguez.

Biblical

A correct explanation of the biblical foundation of this lesson is necessary.

Methodological

Use questions and answers on this topic in order to create a profile of the student's personality type.

The Personality of the Leader
Part 2

4
LESSON

TEACHING OBJECTIVE

The student must understand the need of maturity in order to be a person of good of character.

STUDENT OBJECTIVE

1 The student must be able to explain the features of the leader's personality.

BIBLICAL FOUNDATIONAL REFERENCE

Galatians 5:22-23

1 Timothy 3:1-10

CORRESPONDING BIBLICAL FOUNDATION

Titus 1:5-7

2 Timothy 2:15

1 Thessalonians 5:23

Psalm 139:13

1 Corinthians 13

Galatians 5:16

Romans 5:3-5

Romans 14:17

John 14:27

Luke 6:27-31

Mark 10:17-18

Hebrews 11:1-6

Corinthians 9:24-27

KEY VERSE

"But the fruit of the Spirit is love, joy, peace, patience, kindness, goodness, faithfulness, gentleness and self-control."

(Galatians 5:22-23)

PURPOSE

The world desperately desires leaders who have an honest heart, who can be real examples before others not only in the position of preachers, but also as men who are leaders in their homes; men of truth, people of character. One of the greatest assets of the model of the twelve is the focus on molding the character of a leader.

The purpose of this lesson is to guide the student to effectively understand the concept of personality and its importance in the life of a leader.

1. FEATURES THAT DISTINGUISH THE PERSONALITY OF THE LEADER

Just as personality in general is made up of and defined by various features; the leader's personality is characterized by aspects and features necessary for daily maturity.

A. Enthusiastic

The good leader endeavors to be positive in everything he does, not letting the surrounding circumstances affect him.

"Therefore we do not lose heart. Though outwardly we are wasting away, yet inwardly we are being renewed day by day. For our light and momentary troubles are achieving for us an eternal glory that far outweighs them all. Therefore, we fix our eyes not on what is seen, but on what is unseen. For what is seen is temporary, but what is unseen is eternal". (2 Corinthians 4:16-18)

Do not loose heart

Enthusiasm is a high dose of faith to not look at the circumstances and to be excited about everything we do.

The inner man is renewed

The only way to maintain a daily renewal is to keep our minds open to the direction that the Holy Spirit desires to take. This implies renouncing to the traditional mindset.

Fix the eyes on what is unseen

We must have fellowship with the Spirit of God so that He will open the heavens and we may see in the spiritual realm everything we want Him to transfer to the natural realm.

When your spiritual eyes are opened, you will be amazed by all the things that God has for you, your family and ministry.

You had not conquered this because of fear or ignorance, now, through faith, you can bring them to the natural realm.

B. Of integrity

The good leader inspires trust of his co-workers and of his followers.

A life subjected to the Word is what makes us people of integrity and that is what we then display before others.

"In everything, be an example by doing what is good. In your teaching, show integrity, seriousness and soundness of speech that cannot be condemned, so that those who oppose you may be ashamed because they have nothing bad to say about us" (Titus 2:7-8).

Be an example

It would be much easier to say to people, "do not look at me; look at the Lord." But God chose us as an example of inspiration for many. They are watching what we teach and what we do.

Soundness of speech

Each word that comes from our lips is like a fruit. Our life is like a tree. If we are healed inside, this will be reflected in the value of each word spoken.

When a life is dominated by fear, doubt, or bitterness it will also be reflected in the words spoken.

C.Sure of Himself

Someone who does not believe in himself will never face new challenges because he thinks that if he does, he will fail. If God was bold enough to believe in us, why are we not able to believe in our selves? Men of God were strengthened by what God did in them.

Caleb said, "We should go up and take possession of the land, for we can certainly do it" (Numbers 13:30). Joshua said, "Only do not rebel against the LORD. And do not be afraid of the people of the land, because we will swallow them up. Their protection is gone, but the LORD is with us. Do not be afraid of them" (Numbers 14:9).

David said to Goliath, "This day the LORD will hand you over to me, and I'll strike you down and cut off your head. Today I will give the carcasses of the Philistine army to the birds of the air and the beasts of the earth, and the whole world will know that there is a God in Israel. All those gathered here will know that it is not by sword or spear that the LORD saves; for the battle is the Lord's, and He will give all of you into our hands".(1 Samuel 17:46-47)

D.Trustworthy

This means that the leader takes on small obligations with the same respect as he would a big responsibility, and never thinks of taking personal advantage of what has been entrusted to him, because he has the certainty that in due time he will be exalted.

People can trust him with intricate secrets because he will never disclose them. The hearts, both of the spouse and of the leader, will always be confident (1 Samuel 16:18).

E. Disciplined

In the same way the sprinter trains in order to have a successful race, the believer must work out his spiritual, physical, emotional, and intellectual senses everyday.

He must be very demanding with himself in order to finish his race of faith successfully. "Do you not know that in a race all the runners run, but only one gets the prize? Everyone who competes in the games goes into strict training. They do it to get a crown that will not last; but we do it to get a crown that will last forever. Therefore, I do not run like a man running aimlessly; I do not fight like a man beating the air. No, I beat my body and make it my slave so that after I have preached to others, I myself will not be disqualified for the prize" (1 Corinthians 9:24-27).

F. Perseverance

The apostle Paul said, "The hardworking farmer should be the first to receive a share of the crops" (2 Timothy 2:6). In Japan, the Japanese bamboo, yields its harvest at a staggering slow pace. In fact, it takes years. During this time, the seed has been working hard on its root. After the seventh year, in just six weeks, the great miracle of growth happens when that small seed becomes an awesome bamboo, standing approximately 36 meters high. In your ministerial life you must learn to wait for what the Holy Spirit is doing in the roots of your leadership.
After waiting the right time you will see the development reach unprecedented dimensions.

G. Reproductive

The leader must be able to have a lasting ministry through the people he has trained as leaders. This is crucial for growth to continue. Leading consists of influencing others until they attain their highest potential. As the leader properly influences others, he is molding their character, discovering their worth, and acknowledging their abilities.

CONCLUSION

You are God's masterpiece, Christ's character has been reproduced in you, and you have the ability to be self-controlled. Find out what your personality type is and its characteristics and make the daily effort to submit every area of your life to the leading of Holy Spirit, reflecting the fruit of the Spirit in all you do. This will bring you to a place of authority in the ministry.

APPLICATION

1. Analyze your behavior compared to other people's behavior and try to discover the most predominant features of your personality, until you can define your prevailing temperament.

2. According to Galatians 5: 22 - 23, notice the characteristics, which make up your leadership, if you find any weaknesses in some areas, strengthen them in prayer and with the guidance of your leader.

EVALUATION

Have the student take 5 minutes to write down the weaknesses of his character and how he thinks he can change them.

RECOMMENDATIONS

Bibliographical

Increase your knowledge about this subject by reading the books: SUCCESFUL LEADERSHIP THROUGH THE GOVERNMENT OF 12, and SUBMERGED IN HIS SPIRIT (from the series As Firm As the Rock) by Pastor Cesar Castellanos.

Biblical

The correct explanation of the biblical foundation of this lesson is necessary.

Methodological

Use questions and answers on this topic in order for each student to find out which personality type describes them best.

STUDENTS' ASSIGNMENT

Read chapter 5 of part 1 of the book SUCCESFUL LEADERSHIP THROUGH THE GOVERNMENT OF 12 by Pastor Cesar Castellanos, and make a summary to be handed in to your instructor.
Focus this assignment on your life as a leader.

The Price of Leadership

5
LESSON

TEACHING OBJECTIVE

The student must understand the meaning of paying the price for leadership.

STUDENT OBJECTIVE

1 The student must be able to define what it is "to pay a price".

2 The student must be able to explain the different situations that a leader may go through.

3 The student must be able to explain what God promises those who pay the price.

BIBLICAL FOUNDATIONAL REFERENCE

Luke 14:26-33

CORRESPONDING BIBLICAL FOUNDATION

Luke 9:23

Isaiah 53:3-12

1 Corinthians 11:1

Jeremiah 20:10-12

Acts 6:1-2

Exodus 18:18

2 Corinthians 12:9

Ecclesiastes 3:1

Luke 22:40-43

Psalm 108:13

John 1:11

KEY VERSE

Jesus replied, "No one who puts his hand to the plow and looks back is fit for service in the kingdom of God"
(Luke 9:62)

PURPOSE

Every man must understand that the most important thing is to find his place in the body of Christ where he will have to face great challenges and goals. Moved by His mercy, God chooses to use each one of His children. Then He has to work on their character, sculpting His image and likeness in their lives.

The purpose of this lesson is to teach the students that anyone who desires something of great value should pay a price. Things of little value are soon forgotten but we take good care of what cost us a lot. Although we can speak about a high price in leadership, in reality the Lord Jesus Christ has already paid the price, 2000 years ago. Perhaps the price we can make reference to is to make sure we walk right where the Lord left His footprint.

1.PAYING A PRICE

Many of us feel just like Moses when he came down from the mount where he had experienced God's glory. God gave him the tablets of the law written with His own fingers, but when Moses came down from the mount, he found the people unbridled and surrendered to idolatry. This broke Moses' heart so he broke the tablets of the law. He wanted to renounce the ministry. Every leader has to face difficult situations which cause him to think he is mistaken. He might be tempted to renounce the ministry however there is still a fire that burns in his heart that motivates him to continue. Moses spoke with God and presented all of his own arguments (Exodus 33:12-23).

2.PREPARED TO WITHSTAND

Things will come along the way, that we as leaders will have to withstand with maturity avoiding any damage in other people's lives. Leaders may face the following situations:

a.Criticism

There are two things that deeply affect the servants of God: To see despise and listen to criticism.
The Lord said.

"Who is blind but my servant, and deaf like the messenger I send? Who is blind like the one committed to me, blind like the servant of the LORD? You have seen many things, but have paid no attention; your ears are open, but you hear nothing" (Isaiah 42:19-20).

Jeremiah opposed criticism through faith: "But the LORD is with me like a mighty warrior" (Jeremiah 20:11).

Criticism did not make the apostles change their priorities (Acts 6:1-2).

b.Weariness

The work of the leader is intense and may cause weariness, especially when he does not consider how important it is to delegate. That was the case with Moses in Exodus 18:18. When we find that there is an increase in activities, we can avoid tension by laying it at the Lord's feet; "Come to me, all you who are weary and burdened, and I will give you rest" Matthew 11:28.

c.Time

David told God "My times are in your hands" Psalm 31:15. When our time is redeemed in the presence of God, we work more effectively.
Apparently, the Lord Jesus remained anonymous for thirty years, however in God's timing he began His ministry. In just three and a half years he was able to redeem all of humanity, to found a church and divide the course of history. Let us surrender our lives and ministries to the Lord and He will help us redeem the time.

d.Loneliness

"But Jesus often withdrew to lonely places and prayed"
Luke 5:16
It is necessary to take advantage of those times of loneliness to increase the devotional time with God for the purpose of being strengthened in Him. "Evening, morning, and noon I cry out in distress, and he hears my voice. He ransoms me unharmed from the battle waged against me, even though many oppose me" Psalm 55:17-18.

e.Decisions

"But I determined this with myself, that I would not come again to you in heaviness" (2 Corinthians 2:1).

Paul made the decision to be joyful when visiting the believers in Corinth, and to always lift up their spirits with his words. Every leader must make decisions. When they are made as a result of prayer the outcome will be favorable. David used to consult with God before making any decisions in his life.

f. Rejection

The opposite of acceptance is rejection. Paul was rejected by his own nation. This did not make him give in to their whims, instead he stood firm with no regard for what might occur.

Saul, on the other hand, wanting to win favor with the people, disobeyed God and was cast aside as king. Jesus, being rejected by the Jews, showed mercy to the gentiles. John 1:11-12

3. WHAT THE LORD PROMISES

a. To give us cities and nations

"If the Lord is pleased with us, he will lead us into that land, a land flowing with milk and honey, and will give it to us" (Numbers 14:8).

b. Spiritual authority

"He called His twelve disciples to Him and gave them authority to drive out evil spirits and to heal every disease and sickness" (Matthew 10:1)

c. Prosperity in every area

"Beloved I desire for you to prosper in all things and to have health even as your soul prospers" (3 John 2).

CONCLUSION

Successful leadership is within our reach. We've been born to lead and to positively influence others. No matter the price we have to pay, the effort we have to make or the battles we have to fight, we know that God has called us to His service therefore we will lean completely on Him to keep our soul from anguish. He will cause us to be fruitful in our ministry. It cost Jesus his own life. It will cost us certain amount of sacrifice in the personal and family areas. But God rewards us for this by giving us the nations for us to conquer.

APPLICATION

Paying a price takes in all the areas of your life; examine yourself in order to find out in which areas you need greater surrender and consecration. Take the time to go into fervent prayer until you sense that you are in God's hands. There He will show you His way. Apply the principles that you are learning in this lesson and believe that these will help you to develop your ministry.

EVALUATION

You can take a brief 5-minutes test to evaluate the knowledge the students acquired in this lesson.

RECOMMENDATIONS

Bibliographical

SUCCESFUL LEADERSHIP THROUGH THE GOVERNMENT OF 12 by Pastor Cesar Castellanos

Biblical

Read every verse given in this lesson until you have a clear knowledge of the subject.

Methodological

We suggest you to hand out index cards with the different verses covered in this lesson. Have the student read the verse out loud and explain that scripture with his own words.

STUDENTS' ASSIGNMENT

Read chapters 7 and 8 of part 1 of the book SUCCESFUL LEADERSHIP THROUGH THE GOVERNMENT OF 12 by Pastor Cesar Castellanos, write a summary to be handed in to your instructor.
Focus this assignment to your life as a leader.

Principles for an Excellent Leadership

6

LESSON

TEACHING OBJECTIVE

The student must understand and apply the principles his leadership should go by.

STUDENT OBJECTIVE

1 The student must explain what excellence is.

2 The student must explain what principles a successful leader must live by.

BIBLICAL FOUNDATIONAL REFERENCE

2 Peter 1:3-11

CORRESPONDING BIBLICAL FOUNDATION

Acts 6:3

Acts 11:24

John 3:27

2 Corinthians 4:7

1 Samuel 16:18

Romans 12:3 and 16

Philippians 1:6

Romans 13:1-2

2 Timothy 3:16

Colossians 3:16

1 Thessalonians 4:7-8

1 Timothy 3:1-13

KEY VERSE

"For this very reason, make every effort to add to your faith goodness..."
(2 Peter 1:5)

PURPOSE

The life of a leader must be a life of purpose; with clear and concrete objectives. During our lifetime here on earth we cannot be like a weather vane, moving towards nowhere. We must have an objective to which we should aim towards and a goal that will take us where we want to go. As Christians, we should achieve both internal and external goals.

External goals are based on what we do for God. Inner goals are what we are in God. Many are focused mostly on the outward. They may have good goals that keep them busy all the time such as witnessing, visiting people, training leaders or working on different areas of the ministry. Indeed these things are good, but the main goal is to be focused on what we are in God because we should grow in Christ until His character is reproduced in us.

Jesus said "Be perfect, therefore, as your heavenly Father is perfect" (Matthew 5:48).

After an excellent violin concert, a girl approached the performer and told him "I would give my life to play as you do." The violinist replied, "That is exactly what I did, I gave my life in order to play as I do." Those men who were able to leave a trace in human history had one basic characteristic - they learned to grow in God.

The purpose of this lesson is to help you identify the paths that will lead you to excellence in your life as a leader applying biblical principles whereby you will go beyond mediocrity and contempt as you win and train others in Christ's kingdom.

1.EFFECTIVE LEADERSHIP IS SYNONYMOUS WITH EXCELLENT LEADERSHIP

An effective leader adds excellence to all he does. In Christian leadership, excellence has to do with the essence of the leader himself which is to maintain a fresh, intimate relationship with God. This will be then reproduced in those he is leading.

The leader is excellent in every area of his life.

"Do you not know that in a race all the runners run, but only one gets the prize? Run in such a way as to get the prize" (1 Corinthians 9:24).

No one would start a school to train people to fail in life. Nobody would get married to be the unhappiest person in the world. Everybody longs for a better tomorrow, and many times the cost doesn't matter as long as we find the formula that guarantees success. However we must understand that: "Success was designed for you to obtain it."

It is important for you to understand that the choices of success or failure are within your self. If you accept failure, perhaps it's because, in your family it has been a tradition, or because you don't have a college degree, etc. Well, an attitude like this one says that you are keeping the welcome mat out for this old "guest" to come in and remain as a part of your life. You cannot think this way. You must keep in mind that as a child of God, you have many privileges recorded in the scripture and if you make up your mind to appropriate and claim your rights as a child of God, then the doors will open for you to enter as a conqueror waking towards success.

Napoleon Gil said, "Every thing the human mind is able to imagine can be reached by man." Many times, we do not attain successbecause we never stop to dream. Success believes that, despite the circumstances, you will be able to get by. because we never stop to dream. Success believes that, despite the circumstances, you will be able to get by.

You will find innumerable obstacles trying to block your way, but just consider them as training components that will help you to better deal with those you will be leading.

2. PRINCIPLES OF EXCELLENCE

How can we distinguish an excellent leader from one that is not?

There are many principles associated with excellence. The following are just some of them:

a. Excellence comes from God

"He is the Rock, His works are perfect, and all His ways are just" (Deuteronomy 32:4a).
"A man can receive only what is given him from heaven" (John 3:27).
"But we have this treasure in jars of clay to show that this all-surpassing power is from God and not from us" (2 Corinthians 4:7).

b. Excellence is a characteristic of men of God

"This is what Hezekiah did throughout Judah, doing what was good and right and faithful before the LORD his God. In everything that he undertook in the service of God's temple and in obedience to the law and the commands, he sought his God and worked wholeheartedly. And so he prospered" (2 Chronicles 31:20-21).
"One of the servants answered, "I have seen a son of Jesse of Bethlehem who knows how to play the harp. He is a valiant man and a warrior. He speaks well and is a fine-looking man. And the LORD is with him" (1 Samuel 16:18).

c. Excellence is achieved through effort

"But whatever was once profitable to me I now consider loss for the sake of Christ. What is more, I consider everything a loss compared to the surpassing greatness of knowing Christ Jesus my Lord, for whose sake I have lost all things. I consider them rubbish, that I may gain Christ and be found in him, not having a righteousness of my own that comes from the law, but that which is through faith in Christ the righteousness that comes from God and is by faith" (Philippians 3:7-9).

d. Excellence demands diligence

"Never be found lacking in zeal, but keep your spiritual fervor, serving the Lord" (Romans 12:11).

e. Excellence demands humbleness

"For by the grace given me I say to every one of you, do not think of yourself more highly than you ought, but rather think of yourself with sober judgment, in accordance with the measure of faith God has given you" (Romans 12:3).

f. Excellence seeks perfection in what it does

"Being confident of this, that he who began a good work in you will carry it on to completion until the day of Christ Jesus" (Philippians 1:6).

g. Willingness to face and solve problems

Leadership is a race during which we will experience both happy and sad times. Some of these emotions will be brought on by the people we are leading, so we will need to act with wisdom and sensitivity; continuing in spiritual warfare.

h. Being flexible

The leader must be constant in what he undertakes, but he must also have an open mind towards change. He must be skillful in establishing these changes.

i. Commitment

A high level of excellence in leadership depends on the commitment the leader has towards the people, and that the followers have towards him, disregarding each one's condition or position (1 Samuel 22:2).

CONCLUSION

What we achieve in God will be reflected in what we do for Him. God's excellence is reflected in all His works, and it is our duty as His children to do everything with that same spirit of excellence. Leadership and Excellence must always be related. The Christian leader must long for excellence and to give the very best of himself in the development of the vision that God has revealed for his life and ministry.

APPLICATION

Make a list of those areas you would like to change. Accept that success as yours now, and say as David did, "Surely goodness and mercy will follow me all the days of my life..." (Psalm 23:6).

EVALUATION

Ask the students to do a practical exercise where they can apply what they have learned in this lesson.

RECOMMENDATIONS

Bibliographical

SUCCESFUL LEADERSHIP THROUGH THE GOVERNMENT OF 12 by Pastor Cesar Castellanos

Biblical

Study the biblical references included in this lesson, and the different men of God who did their job with excellence.

Methodological

At the beginning of the class ask the students what principles they think a leader must live by. Write their answers on the board and leave them displayed throughout class time. Compare the answers given as you go on to teach on the principles of a leader. This activity, should take no more than five minutes at the beginning of the class.

STUDENTS' ASSIGNMENT

Read chapter 11 of part 1 of the book SUCCESFUL LEADERSHIP THROUGH THE GOVERNMENT OF 12 by Pastor Cesar Castellanos, and make a summary to be handed in to your instructor.
Focus this paper on your life as a leader.

Dangers in Leadership

7
LESSON

TEACHING OBJECTIVE

The student must understand what the most common dangers in leadership are.

STUDENT OBJECTIVE

1 The student must be able to explain the biblical foundation of each danger in leadership.

2 The student must know and be able to define the antidotes for every one of the dangers.

BIBLICAL FOUNDATIONAL BIBLICAL

1 Timothy 6:11-16

CORRESPONDING BIBLICAL FOUNDATION

1 Samuel 17:34-35

2 Timothy 4:7

Romans 12:3

Numbers 12:16

Numbers 16:1-50

1 Timothy 4:1-3

Joshua 1:9

Joshua 7:21

Proverbs 13:4

Philippians 2:3

2 Corinthians 6:14

Colossians 3:23

2 Timothy 1:7

2 Corinthians 10:4-6

KEY VERSE

"Fight the good fight of the faith. Take hold of the eternal life to which you were called when you made your good confession in the presence of many witnesses"
(1 Timothy 6:12)

PURPOSE

Paul was able to cultivate a good teacher/disciple relationship between him and Timothy. He being the leader advised Timothy on the areas that he should not neglect. He said: "watch your life and doctrine closely, persevere in them, because if you do, you will save both yourself and your hearers" (1 Timothy 4:16).

Paul implies that neither the world, nor the devil will succeed in separating you from Jesus because the greatest danger is yourself. That is why the apostle chastised his own body and submitted it to obedience. The other warning relates to the doctrine; it must be closely observed because that is what will keep you on the right track.

Every leader has to fight tremendous battles if he wishes to successfully fulfill the assigned purpose for which he was called and for his reason of being in this world.

David is a genuine example of a trained man willing to face any kind of danger in order to fulfill what has been assigned to him. On the other hand, Saul, allowed fear in his life and led him to his own destruction.

The objective of this lesson is to inform you of the most common dangers that may affect leadership and assist you with some strategies that will help you to face them and come out victorious.

1.SITUATIONS OF DANGER

A dangerous situation is every thing that threatens to take the life of a person and what a person does, out of order. No leader is exempt from being constantly exposed to these kinds of situations, especially the Christian leader. The enemy is very aware of the leader who has been chosen to use the gospel of Christ to positively influence those who are lost until they are transformed and are rescued from the grip of the enemy.

We can say dangers in leadership arise when we stop depending on God, and start trusting in ourselves or in our own achievements. Paul suggested to Timothy "Fight the good fight of faith, take hold of the eternal life to which you were called when you made your good confession in the presence of many witnesses" (1 Timothy 6:12).

Paul reminds his disciple about:

a) Fighting the battle of faith

There are days when we feel that our level of faith is the highest of the world, but then we feel that faith has faded away leaving us feeling empty again. Why is this? It is because we fight daily in a tremendous battle against spiritual hosts of evil in the heavenly places and these powers have as a goal to weaken the faith of believers. Our victory depends on our relationship with God and with His Word.

b)Taking hold

This means that you must take hold of the eternal life that the Lord has already given to you, without risking your salvation, by flirting with sin.

c) Having made confession

Publicly confessing that Jesus Christ is the Lord of our life is a powerful argument on our behalf in the spiritual world.

2. SOME DANGERS WE MUST BE PREPARED TO FACE

Every leader must be prepared to overcome difficulties and dangers that come about in the life of a Christian. When a leader decides to be committed in the ministry and the vision God has given him, he must be prepared to confront any kind of adversity.

The Lord said, "I will never leave you nor forsake you". "Who will bring any charge against those whom God has chosen? It is God who justifies. But who is he that condemns? Christ Jesus, who died and was raised to life is at the right hand of God and is also interceding for us. Who shall separate us from the love of Christ? Shall trouble or hardship or persecution or famine or nakedness or danger or sword? As it is written:

'For your sake we face death all day long; we are considered as sheep to be slaughtered'. Know, in all these things, we are more than conquerors through him who loved us" (Romans 8:33-37).

Although the enemy tries to accuse us, God has lifted a fence of protection around his servants.

Some dangers the leader faces most frequently are:

A. Pride

"For by the grace given me I say to every one of you, do not think of yourself more highly than you ought, but rather think of yourself with sober judgment, in accordance with the measure of faith God has given you" Romans 12:3.
The antidote: Think of yourself with sober judgment.

B. Murmuring

"Brothers, do not slander one another. Anyone who speaks against his brother or judges him speaks against the law and judges it. When you judge the law, you are not keeping it, but sitting in judgment on it. There is only one Lawgiver and Judge, the one who is able to save and destroy. But who are you to judge your neighbor?" (James 4:11-12).

The antidote: Know that you are not a judge, because in the same way you judge you will be judged.

C. Rebellion

"For rebellion is like the sin of divination, and arrogance like the evil of idolatry.
Because you have rejected the word of the LORD, he has rejected you as king" (1 Samuel 15:23).
The antidote: Absolute obedience to the Word of God.

D. False revelations

"The Spirit clearly says that in latter times some will abandon the faith and follow deceiving spirits and things taught by demons. Such teachings come through hypocrites, whose consciences have been seared as with a hot iron. They forbid people to marry and order them to abstain from certain foods, which God created to be received with thanksgiving by those, who believe and who know the truth. For everything God created is good, and nothing is to be rejected if it is received with thanksgiving, because it is consecrated by the word of God and prayer" (1 Timothy 4:1-5).

The leader has to fight the battle against the spirit of apostasy. Some people neglect grace in order to walk by way of works, they allow a separation between themselves and their spouse even encourage sacrificing nourishment. We must understand that we are not more spiritual by eating or not eating.
The antidote: The Word of God and prayer sanctify everything.

E. Discouragement

"He shall say, hear, O Israel, today you are going into battle against your enemies. Do not be fainthearted or afraid; do not be terrified or give way to panic before them. For the LORD your God is the one who goes with you to fight for you against your enemies to give you victory" (Deuteronomy 20:3-4).

Discouragement comes when we have to face great challenges or responsibilities and it is when we tend to fix our eyes on the circumstances instead of on God. This causes:

a) Our heart to faint.
b) Fear to come.
c) Confusion to enter.
d) Discouragement to take over.

The antidote is the promise that:

e) God is with us.
f) He fights for us.
g) He saves us.

The battle is won within us first for what we believe in our heart and confess with our mouth will come to pass.

F. Negligence

"Lazy hands make a man poor, but diligent hands bring wealth. He who gathers crops in summer, is a wise son, but he who sleeps during harvest is a disgraceful son" (Proverbs 10:4-5).

The negligent one is the person who sees the spiritual need of his city but prefers to postpone his work; this produces ministerial poverty.

The antidote: be diligent and understand that we are living in times of great spiritual harvest. If we believe it and act, God will enrich our ministries.

G. Envy

"And I saw that all labor and all achievement spring from man's envy of his neighbor. This too is as meaningless as chasing after the wind" (Ecclesiastes 4:4).

Envy is the result of a frustration. When people hear about the success of others, they tend to become uncomfortable and can incur murmuring, criticism, and an afflicted spirit.

The antidote:

a) Excellence in everything, because when you arrive at it, frustration disappears which is what produces discomfort when others make progress

b) Enjoy other people's success, as if it was yours. This will renew your spirit.

H. Covetousness

"I was enraged by his sinful greed; I punished him, and hid my face in anger, yet he kept on in his willful ways. I have seen his ways, but I will heal him; I will guide him and restore comfort to him, creating praise on the lips of the mourners in Israel. Peace, peace, to those far and near," says the LORD. "And I will heal them" Isaiah 57:17-19

Covetousness causes:

a) God to be enraged.
b) You to be hurt.
c) God to hide His face from you.
d) God to become indignant about you.

The antidote:

e) Repent truly.
f) Let go of your own ways in order to walk in His paths.
g) Allow Him to heal the wounds form your past.

h)Accept Him as the pastor of your life.
i) Change your language and proclaim peace.

I. Fear

"Fear of man will prove to be a snare, but whoever trusts in the LORD is kept safe" Proverbs 29:25.

Fear is the result of a wounded heart, it paralyzes man in every decision he has to make. Saul is a great example of the disastrous effects of fear.

The antidote: Paul said "For God did not give us a spirit of timidity, but a spirit of power, of love and of self-discipline" (2 Timothy 1:7).
As children of God, we have to reject fear in all its manifestations because fear's mission is to steal, kill and destroy.
You can do the following prayer:

"Father I repent for having allowed fear in my life, I renounce fear with all my strength and I rebuke it from my life. I believe that at the cross Jesus took all of my fear and set me free from that curse. I accept the spirit of power and self-control given by Jesus to me, and I know that Jesus is by my side as a powerful giant, and He will always fight for me, Amen".

CONCLUSION

When you know the rules of justice and the warnings of danger, you know that by simply obeying, you will be protected from evil, because it is written.

"Then no harm will befall you, no disaster will come near your tent. For he will command his angels to guard you in all your ways; they will lift you up in their hands, so that you will not strike your foot against a stone" (Psalm 91:10-12).

Paul said "For if you possess these qualities in increasing measure, they will keep you from being ineffective and unproductive in your knowledge of our Lord Jesus Christ" (2 Peter 1:8).

APPLICATION

1. Always focus on remaining in first place, not allowing anything in your life to disqualify you. Identify what hinders the development of your spiritual life the most and pluck it out of your life!

2. Practice spiritual warfare on a daily basis, for the sake of your life, your family, and the ministry.

3. Appropriate the victory given by Jesus at the cross of Calvary, and make it yours every day, for if you are free you can help others.

EVALUATION

At the end of class, ask the students to write down what dangers they are falling in; then pray for them.

RECOMMENDATIONS

Bibliographical

SUCCESFUL LEADERSHIP THROUGH THE GOVERNMENT OF 12 by Pastor Cesar Castellanos.

Biblical

Read all the biblical passages given in this lesson in order to have a better understanding of every danger.

Methodological

Take a test.

STUDENTS' ASSIGNMENT

Read chapter 6 of part 1 of the book SUCCESFUL LEADERSHIP THROUGH THE GOVERNMENT OF 12 by Pastor Cesar Castellanos. Write a summary to be handed in to your instructor. Focus this assignment on your life as a leader.

Types of Leadership

8

LESSON

TEACHING OBJECTIVE

The student must understand the types of leadership.

STUDENT OBJECTIVE

1 The student must define the types of leadership.

2 The student must describe what we must take into account in order to achieve a leadership of success.

BIBLICAL FOUNDATIONAL REFERENCE

Matthew 20:25-28

CORRESPONDING BIBLICAL FOUNDATION

1 Corinthians 1:11

2 Timothy 2:2

Romans 13:1

2 Timothy 3:1-5

Titus 2:7-8

Matthew 20:28

KEY VERSE

"Not so with you. Instead, whoever wants to become great among you must be your servant"
(Matthew 20:26)

PURPOSE

We have mentioned many excellent aspects of leadership, but it is very important to remember that there are different types of leaders. This depends on how they use their authority and the motivation that takes them to lead others.

The Bible says that in a vineyard, there are different kinds of workers (see Matthew 20:1-16) and this can be compared to the work of God where we find several kinds of leaders.

The important thing is to find the perfect balance to develop the leadership God wants, which will contribute to the spreading of the gospel and the growth of the church.

Making leaders is one of the main challenges of our church. We do it convinced that God desires an active church prepared to gather the harvest of souls, men and women who open their hearts to Jesus daily.

"Then he said to his disciples, "The harvest is plentiful but the workers are few. Ask the Lord of the harvest, therefore, to send out workers into his harvest field" Matthew 9:37-38

The workers God requires are those who will grow to the stature of an effective leadership.

This lesson may be considered complementary to lesson number one; the goal is to guide the student to select an effective leadership in order to attain multiplication.

1.LEVELS OF LEADERSHIP

John Maxwell develops an interesting analysis about the levels of leadership:

A.Position

This is the lowest level in leadership, the only influence this leader has, comes from a title. People follow the leader because they have to.

B.Permission

This is when the leader succeeds in making people work for him when they are not obliged to do it. People follow the leader because they want to.

C.Production

This level is when things begin to happen, good things. People follow the leader because of what he has done for the organization.

D.Human development

A leader is great not because of his power, but because of the ability to bring others into a higher position. People follow the leader for what he has done for them.

E.Personality

This is the highest level of all. People follow the leader because of what he is and means to them.
(Taken from the book: Develop the Leader within You. John Maxwell, page 26)

In order to attain to the level of personality, keep in mind these things:

a.BE A BROKEN PERSON

An effective leader is one who has achieved his maximum potential, and is able to give the best results becoming an example to others.
The born leader is a person of influence who has followers, directly or indirectly. However, God has to deal with each one of those He has chosen, taking them through a process of purification, removing from their lives anything that is a hindrance in their ministry. Every time one tries to lean on something that is not God, the Lord intervenes making one die to it.

Then, people are ready to fulfill the divine purpose. Let us look at some examples of those men of God who were absolutely broken by God's power through different circumstances:

1.Abraham

God ask him what he loved the most, his own son. Genesis 22.

2.Jacob

He has to fight with an angel during one of his most difficult moments. He had found out that his brother Esau was coming after him with four hundred men. This made Jacob seek God most desperately. He grabbed the angel and said he would not let him go until he received his blessing. In that prayer Jacob saw God face to face. Afterwards, he saw God's face again as he encountered his brother Esau.

3.Moses

He has the revelation of the burning bush, which is not burnt. When he gets closer in order to see such a marvelous thing, he hears the voice of the Lord who says, "Moses, take off your shoes because this place is holy". The fire of God's holiness purifies Moses' heart and God can entrust him with the deliverance of His people.

b.BE THE LEADER THAT INFLUENCES BY LIVING A LIFE OF FAITH

Now faith is being sure of what we hope for and certain of what we do not see" (Hebrews 11:1).

Everyone who desires to have a successful ministry must always live in the dimension of faith, because through it our relationship with God is strengthened and we are able to accomplish all our dreams.

c.BE A LEADER LED BY THE HOLY SPIRIT

The Lord Jesus, referring to the ministry of the Holy Spirit said, "He will bring glory to me by taking from what is mine and making it known to you. All that belongs to the Father is mine. That is why I said the Spirit will take from that which is mine and make it known to you" John 16:14-15.

We can see that the Holy Spirit is the legal representative of God on earth. As long as Jesus is revealed to us and we understand the Scriptures, the Lord is glorified; we must be sensitive to His voice. Seek the Lord daily for guidance in all things, not just in personal matters but also in matters of ministry.

d.BE A LEADER OF PRAYER

Let us think for a moment. If the Lord had to depend on prayer, what a need we have to pray! The best sermons any leader could preach are those, which have been prepared in the secret room of prayer.

CONCLUSION

In order to obtain something of great value, a great price has to be paid. Being called to serve God is a tremendous privilege, but we have to fulfill the previously mentioned requirements.

The kind of leadership you aspire to have is all up to you. An easy leadership which demands no effort on our part will produce mediocre results; an effective leadership is the one in which the leader has developed his maximum potential, obtaining the best results, becoming an example for others, but all because of the price that was paid.

APPLICATION

Let these principles dwell in your life permanently, allowing the Spirit of God to break you maintaining a disciplined life of prayer and living in the dimension of faith. Let the Spirit of God guide you in every step making you the person God wants to use to demonstrate His love and His power.

EVALUATION

At the end of the class, ask your students what kind of leader they want to be, and clear any doubts that could prevent them from becoming that leader.

RECOMMENDATIONS

Bibliographical

SUCCESFUL LEADERSHIP THROUGH THE GOVERNMENT OF 12 by Pastor Cesar Castellanos

Biblical

Read all the scriptures relayed in this lesson in order to have a better understanding of every kind of danger.

Methodological

Take a test.

STUDENTS' ASSIGNMENT

Read chapters 4 and 5 of part 2 of the book SUCCESFUL LEADERSHIP THROUGH THE GOVERNMENT OF 12 by Pastor Cesar Castellanos, and make a summary to be handed in to your instructor.
Focus this paper on your life as a leader.

Practical Advices for Preaching Part 1

9

LESSON

TEACHING OBJECTIVE

The student must know the different preaching techniques.

STUDENT OBJECTIVE

1 The student must be able to define what preaching is.

2 The student must describe how to prepare an outline for preaching.

BIBLICAL FOUNDATIONAL REFERENCE

Ephesians 4:12-16

CORRESPONDING BIBLICAL FOUNDATION

2 Corinthians 11:2-6

Philippians 4:8-9

Joshua 1:8

Psalm 32:8-9

Isaiah 59:21

Daniel 12:3

Hosea 4:6

Hosea 4:14

Habakkuk 2:14

John 5:39

2 Timothy 3:16, 17

KEY VERSE

"Instead, speaking the truth in love, we will in all things grow up into him who is the Head, that is, Christ" **(Ephesians 4:15)**

PURPOSE

One of the greatest privileges that anyone can have in the world is to be a preacher of the gospel. It is equivalent to being chosen by God to represent him in this world.

Every time the leader teaches or preaches he is nourishing people spiritually (this is up to the level of responsibility that he has). When the leader really desires to do God's work, he will live with great compassion towards those the Lord has entrusted him with. They become like spiritual babies of whom the leader takes care of, feeding them excellent spiritual nutrition.

Through this lesson, you will be able to find some key aspects to become an effective and compassionate communicator of truth and of the word of life, which will bring salvation to those who listen to it.

1.WHAT DOES PREACHING CONSIST OF?

Preaching the Word is more than knowing how to give a message. Anybody can learn a lesson by heart and repeat it, but the preaching of the gospel goes beyond communicating theoretical concepts. The preacher is like a channel through which the river of life flows with the message of God. God is very careful that his river only flows through properly prepared channels and for this reason God has to sanctify the life of the one who is going to be His spokesperson.

Many preachers have trained themselves to preach excellent messages thinking this was the way the needs of the people would be met; without them understanding that more than that is required. Every teaching we give should supply their needs. When someone goes to a meeting, they do it because they are hoping to receive the answer to their needs from God and if they don't find that they will simply begin to look for another place where the power of God manifests itself through faith meeting their needs.

All those who have lived distant from God have fallen into the trap of the enemy. He has hurt them in different ways. That is the reason why the first ones to arrive to your group will be the most needy.

"All those who were in distress or in debt or discontented gathered around him, and he became their leader. About four hundred men were with him" (1 Samuel 22:2).

God entrusts them to you for you to form them until they become courageous, spiritual warriors. To that respect, Paul said, "Do your best to present yourself to God as one approved, a workman who does not need to be ashamed and who correctly handles the word of truth" (2 Timothy 2:15).

2. PREPARATION FOR PREACHING

Preparation for preaching must begin in the spiritual area of the preacher's life. The person, who desires to be used by God in sharing His message to a congregation, must live a life of much daily prayer (Ephesians 6:18a), and must be in direct contact with the Word of God (Isaiah 59:21).

The following suggestions will help you to prepare a message according to God's purpose:

- Have the habit of constantly studying the Bible by books, chapters and verses.
- Prepare the message, applying it to your own life.
- Memorize as many scriptures as you can. This will help you handle the message with authority in public.
- Use the dictionary in order to learn with accuracy the meaning of some terms and their synonyms.

Outline the sermon according to the following guidelines:

A. Title

Choose a title that is brief and focused on the objective of the sermon.

B. Objective

Seek God in order to receive the Rhema word for the group. Preach with all your faith, knowing that the message will meet the needs for the spiritual nourishment of the listeners.

C. Introduction

Use an interesting and catchy illustration related to the preaching that will get the attention of the listener.

F. Text

Specify the main biblical reference. You may memorize it in order to be able to quote it time and again without reading.

G. Main divisions

Make a sequence of 3 to 5 points (some experts recommend that is enough in order to fulfill the purpose of the teaching) suitable for the audience to understand and remember.

H. Conclusion

Briefly summarize what was preached making sure the listener remembers the different points mentioned.

I. Application

If the sermon does not have an application to an actual situation it will lose the primary essence which is to make the promises of the Word become life for the people.

CONCLUSION

The leader must be prepared to communicate the message of Christ in an efficient way. His life is an opene letter read by the whole world. His preaching will be the only hope that some will have to reach salvation. His faith will be the example many will want to attain for themselves. His prayer life will be his spiritual strength.

APPLICATION

1. Have the rhema word from God for your life.
2. Share with others what God ministered to you.
3. Always speak words of faith and hope.

Practical Advices for Preaching Part 2

10
LESSON

TEACHING OBJECTIVE

The student must know the different preaching techniques.

STUDENT OBJECTIVE

1 The student must be able to define what preaching is.

2 The student must describe how to prepare an outline for preaching.

BIBLICAL FOUNDATIONAL REFERENCE

Ephesians 4:12-16

CORRESPONDING BIBLICAL FOUNDATION

2 Corinthians 11:2-6

Philippians 4:8-9

Joshua 1:8

Psalm 32:8-9

Isaiah 59:21

Daniel 12:3

Hosea 4:6

Hosea 4:14

Habakkuk 2:14

John 5:39

2 Timothy 3:16, 17

KEY VERSE

"Instead, speaking the truth in love, we will in all things grow up into him who is the Head, that is, Christ"
(Ephesians 4:15)

PURPOSE

One of the greatest privileges that anyone can have in the world is to be a preacher of the gospel. It is equivalent to being chosen by God to represent him in this world.

Every time the leader teaches or preaches he is nourishing people spiritually (this is up to the level of responsibility that he has). When the leader really desires to do God's work, he will live with great compassion towards those the Lord has entrusted him with. They become like spiritual babies of whom the leader takes care of, feeding them excellent spiritual nutrition.

Through this lesson, you will be able to find some key aspects to become an effective and compassionate communicator of truth and of the word of life, which will bring salvation to those who listen to it.

1.Managing the Scriptures

- Select the key text based on the general topic.

- Examine the context. Get thoroughly acquainted with the context. Take account of the previous and following verses of the main text.

- Take into account the prevailing characteristics and topics in the passage. This part will help you structure the main divisions of the sermon.

- Consider the scriptures in a general way, so that you do not overlook other passages which are closely related to the principal subject of the message you are preparing.

2.General considerations for the opening of the message

· Be yourself

Do not try to imitate another speaker.

· Be the first one to live what you preach

The listeners are looking at you as an example worthy to imitate.

· Be clear, concise and precise

The good speaker is the one who makes easy what is diffi cult; what is confusing he makes it simple, and leaves a clear teaching in the minds of the people.

· Speak in a natural way

Speak as you do at home. Do not shout because the audience may feel rebuked. Do not speak too low because the people may fall asleep. Always speak with all your heart.

CONCLUSION

The leader must be prepared to communicate the message of Christ in an efficient way. His life is an opene letter read by the whole world. His preaching will be the only hope that some will have to reach salvation. His faith will be the example many will want to attain for themselves. His prayer life will be his spiritual strength.

APPLICATION

1. Have the rhema word from God for your life.
2. Share with others what God ministered to you.
3. Always speak words of faith and hope.

WORKSHOP

Ask your students to take a sheet of paper and a pencil and draft an outline of a sermon. The teacher will choose the subject. Remember that the workshop is helpful, so be available to guide your students through every one of their questions.

Notice: at the beginning of this lesson be sure to plan your time precisely. Maximum duration of the workshop: 30 minutes.

7 Truths that will Strengthen your Marriage
Cesar Castellanos D.
Developing a Supernatural Leadership
G12
Cesar Castellanos D.
Dream
and you will win the world
Cesar Castellanos D.
Successful Leadership through the Government of
G12
Cesar Castellanos
The Ladder of Success
School of Leaders
Doctrine
Seminar
Find the tools for Multiplication
www.g12bookstore.com
USA (305)9401499 Miami,Fl.